Let's Draw!

5: What Comes Next?

Colin Caket and Leon Baxter

Collins
in association with
 Belitha Press

Let's draw together . . .

Drawing is fun so why not join in! This series of books will help you to put on paper the things you see around you, and the things you see in your head. There is no **right** way to draw – every artist has his or her own way of doing things. And so do you. These books will help you to find the way **you** like to draw, and give you some hints about what makes your picture 'work'.

I hope all the suggestions, ideas and games in **Let's Draw** will inspire you to create amazing pictures. Once you make a picture you like, you will be keen to draw more and more. Experiment! Use wax crayons and paint together – see what happens. Instead of colouring an area with just one coloured pencil, try two or more, or mix your pencil lines with areas of felt-tip colour. There are all sorts of things you can do.

Don't worry if your picture is not exactly how you want it to be – have another go. It's much better to do *lots* of practise drawings, than to attempt one precious masterpiece. But remember – don't waste paper, fill it to every corner and use both sides of your page.

If you **do** make lots of pictures your drawing will improve. Look at the pictures that you like and decide *why* you like them. Be encouraged by them and draw some more. Solving problems is easy and exciting.

Things you will need:

coloured pencils	paint
crayons	sticky coloured paper
pastels	lots of drawing paper (white and coloured)
felt-tip pens	

Have a good time!

Leon Baxter

First published 1988 by William Collins Sons and Co Ltd
in association with Belitha Press Limited,
31 Newington Green, London N16 9PU
Text and illustrations in this format copyright © Belitha Press 1988
Text and illustrations copyright © the estate of Colin Caket and Leon Baxter 1988
Art Director: Treld Bicknell   Editor: Carol Watson
All rights reserved. No part of this publication may be reproduced in any form whatsoever without the permission of the publishers and the copyright holders.
ISBN 0 00 197710 5
Typesetting by Chambers Wallace, London
Printed in Italy

Look carefully. Find what comes next and fill in the blanks.

A

What comes next?

Draw in the missing pictures.

What happens next?

Watch how the man's legs change.

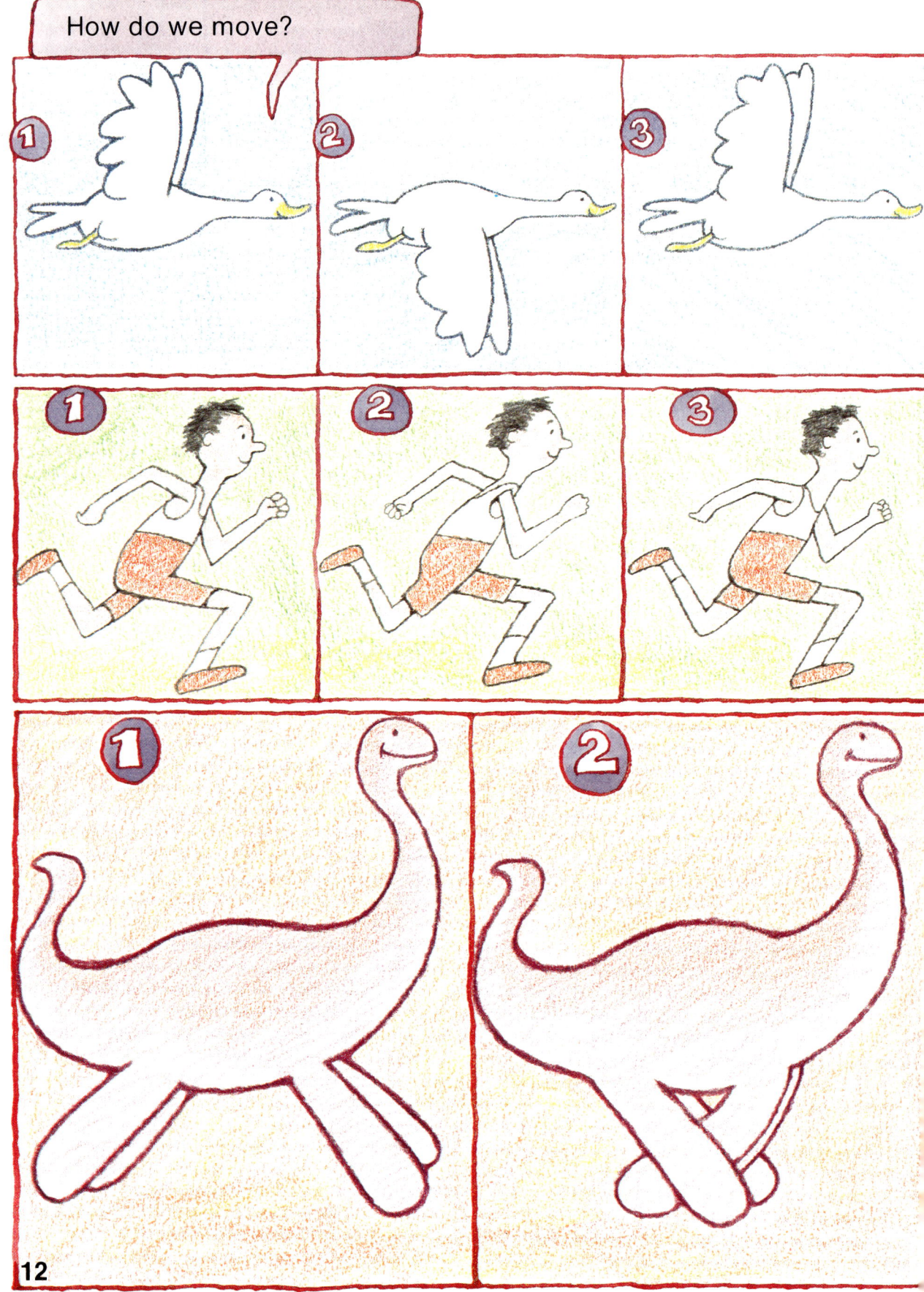

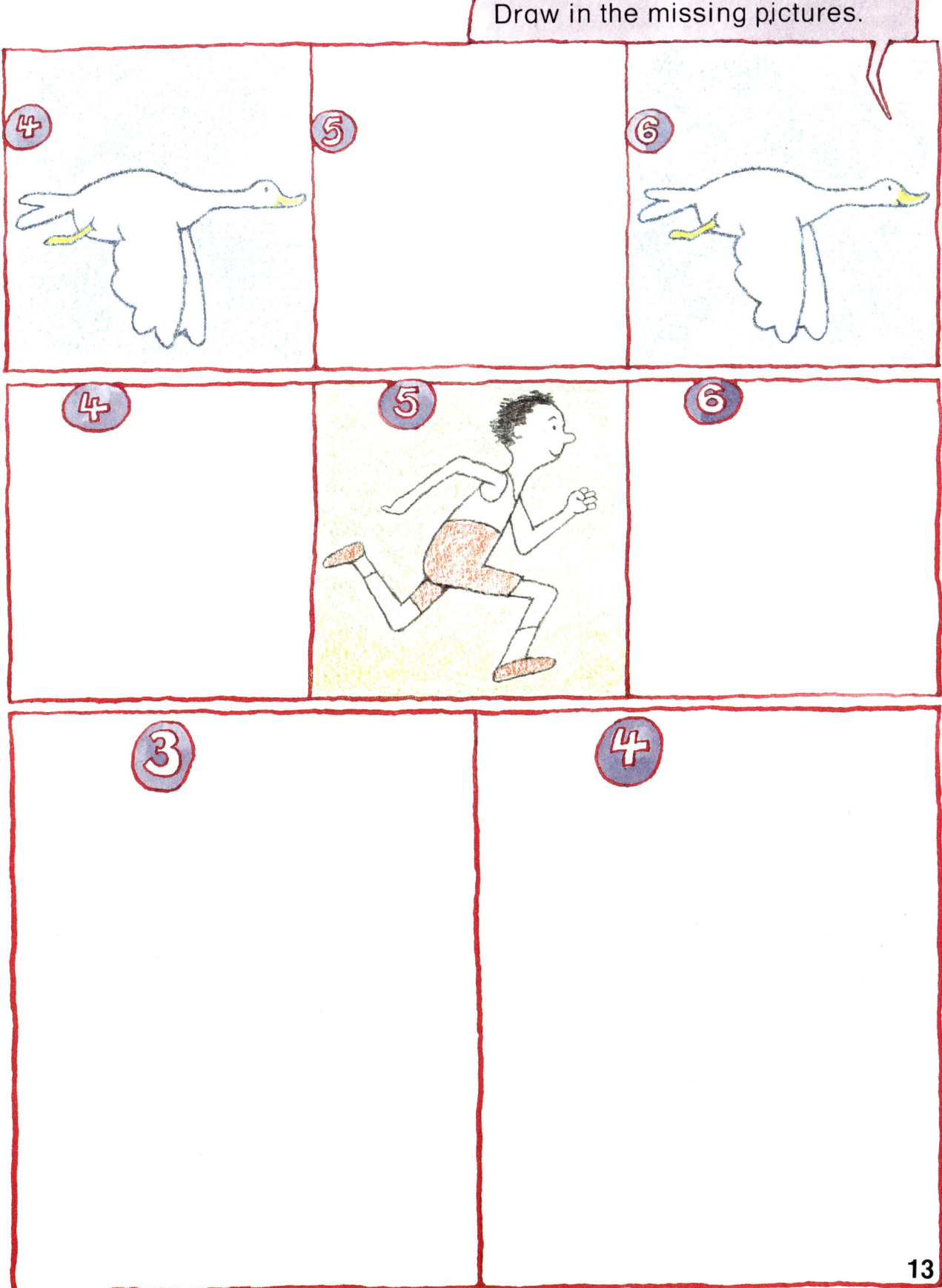

Playtime! What will the children do next?

Can you draw what the robot is doing in the squares below?

Flick Books

On the page opposite there are two drawings of a little girl. You can make her come to life by putting her in a flick book.

First make a pad of stiff paper or thin card. (You need at least twelve pages so the book will be easy to flick.)

Next trace or copy drawing **A** onto one end of a piece of paper.

Then trace drawing **B** onto the next piece.

Repeat this pattern on all your other pages. Now clip the pages together at the opposite end to your drawings.
You can use a bulldog clip, staples or a split pin.

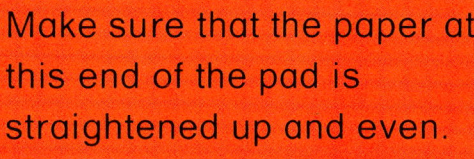

Make sure that the paper at this end of the pad is straightened up and even.

Now hold the book at the clipped end and flick the pages.

The little girl is skipping!

Try this page size to start with.

A

B

You can make flick books in many sizes. Draw pictures of different actions, but keep the movement simple.

You can make your own simple movie by using the disc on the opposite page.

First trace the disc onto stiff card. Carefully trace round the edge of each dog. Now use a black felt-tip pen to colour in the little dogs. (If you find it easier you can cut round the disc on page 23 when you have finished the book.)

Next cut out the disc, the dotted slits in the disc and the hole in the middle. You may need an adult to help you, because it is important that the edges are very neat.

Put a pencil through the hole in the middle of the disc with the blank side towards you. Hold it up to a mirror, look through the slots and gently spin the disc. Your little dog will be running!

Making Movies

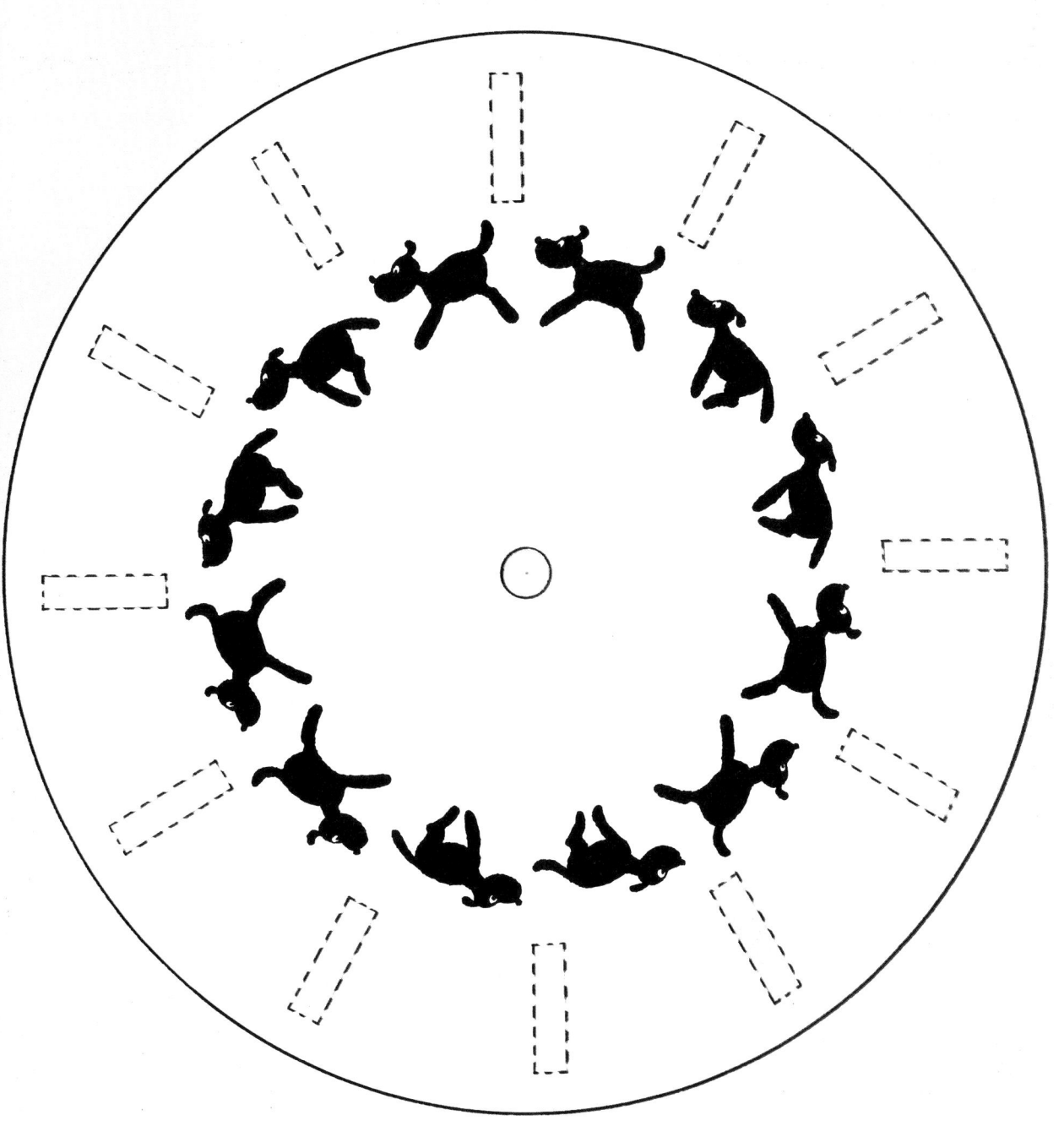

You can make other discs and draw your own pictures. Simple black shapes will work best.